Crafts From Your Favorite

Nursery Rhymes

by KATHY ROSS

Illustrated by Elaine C̶a̶r̶v̶i̶n̶

The Millbrook Press   Brookfield,

Library of Congress Cataloging-in-Publication Data
Ross, Kathy.
Crafts from your favorite nursery rhymes / Kathy Ross ;
illustrated by Elaine Garvin.
p. cm.
Summary: Provides instructions for twenty easy-to-make crafts based on nursery rhymes,
including a Jack and Jill party hat, an old woman's shoe magnet, and a runaway dish and spoon
puppet.
ISBN 0-7613-2523-9 (lib. bdg.) ISBN 0-7613-1589-6 (pbk.)
1. Handicraft—Juvenile literature. [1. Handicraft.]
I. Garvin, Elaine, ill. II. Title.
TT160 .R7133 2003   745.5—dc21   2001044665

Published by The Millbrook Press, Inc.
2 Old New Milford Road
Brookfield, Connecticut 06804
www.millbrookpress.com

Contents

For my Julianna Jellybean
KR

To my sweet Ellie, with lots of love from Gramma.
EG

Introduction

There is something about the lilting rhythms of nursery rhymes that imprint themselves on a child's mind. The stories told by the verses are often nonsensical, and yet decades after childhood we adults can easily remember what happened to Humpty Dumpty, or what the dish ran away with.

So, if children are going to be carrying these verses with them throughout life, why not enhance the memories? Hands-on projects are not only a wonderful way to spend time with a child but they also help foster manual dexterity and enhance creativity. And, as an additional bonus, the child will have created a decorative or useful object that can be displayed with pride.

I've had many hours of fun making these projects with my classes. I hope you will enjoy them too.

Kathy Ross

"Little Bo Peep has lost her sheep…"

Little Bo Peep Sleeve Puppet

Here is what you need:

construction paper in the skin tone of your choice

yarn for hair

an old long-sleeved man's shirt with button cuffs

white glue

ribbon and trims

ruler

markers

brown pipe cleaner

scissors

two wiggle eyes

artificial flowers

Here is what you do:

1 Cut one sleeve off the shirt about 12 inches (30 cm) from the cuff to use as the body for the puppet.

CUT

2 Cut a 6-inch (15-cm) circle of construction paper for the face. Push the center of the paper up through the sleeve to the end of the cuff to form a face, with the cuff of the sleeve surrounding the face to look like a bonnet. Glue the face in place.

GLUE SPACE BETWEEN CUFF AND PAPER

3 Use the markers to draw a mouth above the place where the cuff buttons. Draw a nose and rosy cheeks on the face. Glue on the two wiggle eyes. Cut some yarn bits and glue them around the face for hair.

4 Glue a ruffle of trim around the cuff bonnet. Glue a pretty bow under the chin for the tie on the bonnet.

5 Curve one end of the pipe cleaner to make Bo Peep's staff. Tie a bow on the staff and tuck in some artificial flowers.

6 Cut two hands for the puppet from construction paper. Glue the two hands on the front of the puppet with the tips touching. Glue a piece of trim on the wrist of each hand to look like the cuffs of the dress. Tuck the staff in behind the hands to look like the puppet is holding it.

7 Glue more trim around the bottom of the dress of the puppet.

8 Put the Bo Peep puppet over your hand and take her to find her lost sheep.

"This little piggy went
'wee, wee, wee, wee' all the way home."

Squealing Piggy

Here is what you need:

- two identical cups
- pink sock 
- two-holed button 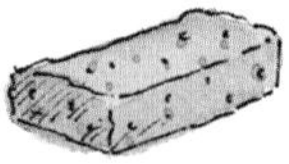
- pink embroidery thread
- pink pipe cleaner
- cellulose sponge 
- ruler
- white glue
- water
- scissors
- two wiggle eyes

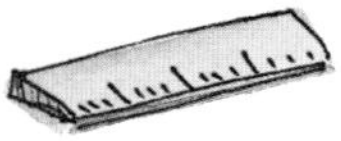

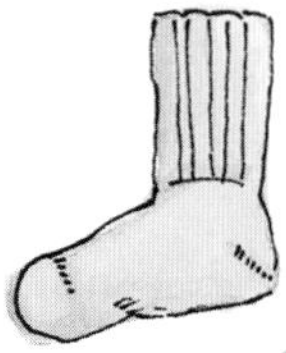

Here is what you do:

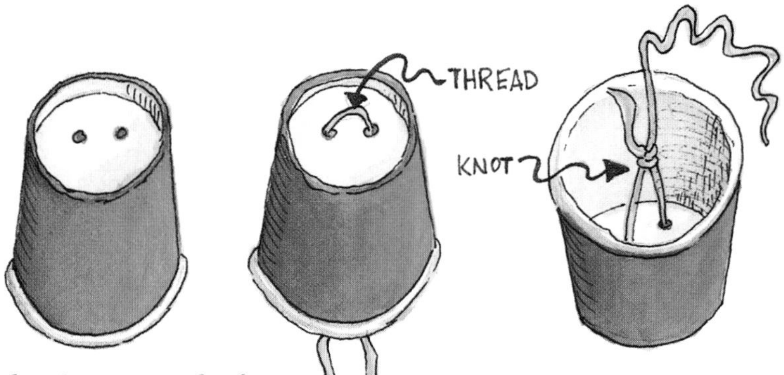

1 Poke two small holes in the bottom of one cup.

2 Cut a 2-foot (60-cm) length of the pink embroidery thread. Tie one end of the thread through the two holes in the cup so that the thread hangs down out of the cup.

THREAD

KNOT

SLOP SHOP MARKET

SALE

3 Cut the toe end from the pink sock, just in front of the heel. If you do not have a pink sock, use a white one, then paint the piggy pink.

CUT

4 Slip the sock over the second cup to cover it for the body of the pig. Fold the edge of the sock down inside the cup, then slip the second cup into the first cup to hold the sock in place.

FOLD SOCK INSIDE

5 Wrap a 3-inch (8-cm) piece of the pink pipe cleaner around your finger to curl it for a tail for the pig. Dip one end of the tail in the glue and slip it between the two cups to attach it to the pig.

GLUE

SLIP BETWEEN CUPS

6 Cut two triangle-shaped ears for the pig from the heel portion of the sock. Pleat the ears at the center of the bottom of the triangles and glue each ear to the bottom of the cup across from the tail.

7 Glue on the two wiggle eyes below the ears. Glue on the button below the eyes for a nose for the pig.

PULL DOWN WET SPONGE

8 To make the piggy squeal, moisten a small piece of the cellulose sponge with water and pull it down the string hanging from the bottom of the inner cup. Have fun experimenting with the squeals to find just the right noise for your piggy to make.

All mine

Where's Mine?

FEED ME!

Wee, wee, wee

"There was an old woman who lived in a shoe . . ."

Old Woman's Shoe Magnet

Here is what you need:

brown, yellow, and red construction paper scraps

black marker

scissors

brown fat marker cap

white glue

string

piece of sticky-back magnet

Here is what you do:

1 Fold a scrap of brown construction paper in half. Use the marker to draw a foot for the shoe. The marker cap will form the upper part of the old-fashioned shoe, which looks like a boot.

FOLD   CUT

2 Cut out the foot part of the shoe through both pieces of paper so that you have two sides to the shoe.

3 Glue the back part of the paper shoe around the end of the marker cap, then glue the two sides of the paper shoe together.

GLUE TOGETHER

GLUE

WRAP

4 Cut a door and windows for the shoe from the yellow paper scraps. Add details with the marker. Glue the door and windows to one side of the shoe.

5 Fold a scrap of red paper in half and cut a tiny two-sided roof for the shoe. Glue the roof to the top of the shoe.

FOLD

GLUE BOW TO BOOT

6 Tie a piece of string into a bow. Glue the bow to the top of the shoe to look like a tied shoelace.

7 Put a piece of sticky-back magnet on the back of the shoe.

Would you like to live in a shoe?

SHINE SHOES

MILK CHEESE BREAD

A+

(11)

"Jack and Jill went up the hill . . ."

Jack and Jill Party Hat

Here is what you need:

old party hat

green poster paint and a paintbrush

scissors

construction paper scraps

white glue

green yarn

markers

tiny artificial flowers

Here is what you do:

1 Paint the party hat green for the hill.

2 Cut the point off to create a small opening at the top of the hat.

CUT TIP OFF

GREEN

3 Cut a small well from construction paper. Glue the well to the topside of the hat.

4 Cut a 2-foot (60-cm) length of the green yarn. Thread the yarn down through the hole in the tip of the hat. Tie the two ends together leaving the loop of yarn loose enough to slide freely up and down the hat.

5 Fold a piece of construction paper in half. Use the markers to draw Jack and Jill about 2 inches (5 cm) tall and with their feet at the fold in the paper. Cut around the figures without cutting through the fold in the paper.

6 Slip the back fold of the paper under the yarn loop on the hat, then glue the front and back sides together to attach the figures to the loop.

7 Glue the tiny artificial flowers on the hat hill to decorate it.

Move Jack and Jill up the hill, then quickly down again, by pulling on the yarn loop.

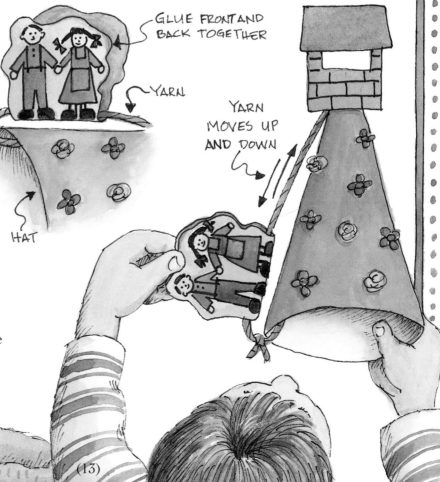

"Put her in a pumpkin shell,
and there he kept her very well."

Peter's Wife in a Pumpkin Shell

Pumpkin Bread

Here is what you need:

markers

two discarded compact discs (CDs)

orange and green construction paper

scissors

white glue

old glove

yarn bits for hair

two tiny wiggle eyes

masking tape

Here is what you do:

1 Trace around the CDs on the orange paper. Cut both orange circles out. Glue an orange circle over the printed side of one CD.

GLUE TOGETHER

2 Cut through the hole in the center of the CD. Use the markers to draw a window around the hole in the CD. Add details to the orange paper to make it look like a pumpkin house.

CUT OUT

3 Cut a stem for the pumpkin from the green paper and glue it to the top of the pumpkin.

4 Cut a finger from the old glove to make the wife.

5 Glue on yarn bits for hair and two wiggle eyes.

6 Use the markers to add a nose, mouth, and rosy cheeks.

BACK OF PUMPKIN TOP

GLUE TO BOTTOM CD

7 Use masking tape to hinge the back of the top of the pumpkin to the second CD so that it will fold down behind the pumpkin.

8 Cover the inside surface of the second CD with the second orange circle.

TAPE INSIDE PUPPET

9 Use masking tape to attach the finger puppet wife to the back of the pumpkin CD so that she is peeking out the window hole.

To use the puppet, slip your middle finger into the finger puppet and support the pumpkin shell with your remaining fingers.

"Patty cake, patty cake, baker's man . . ."

Patty Cake Baby

Here is what you need:

fabric or net

pencil

wooden craft bead with wide hole

markers

scissors

white glue

yarn bits for hair

thin ribbon

clamp clothespin

shoulder pad

Here is what you do:

1 Cut a 6-inch (15-cm) circle of fabric for the dress for the baby. Dip the center of the fabric in glue and use the pencil to push the gluey fabric up into the hole in the bead.

← BEAD

GLUE
← FABRIC

TIP OF PENCIL

2 Use the markers to draw a face on the bead.

3 Glue yarn bits in the top of the bead for hair. Make a bow from the thin ribbon. Glue the bow to the hair of the baby.

4 Clamp the clothespin around the dress at the neck of the baby to look like arms.

5 Cut a hole in the center of the shoulder pad. Slide the ends of the clothespin through the hole so that it looks like the baby is lying in a little cradle bed.

Squeeze the ends of the clothespin behind the shoulder pad to make the baby "patty cake."

SQUEEZE

"Four-and-twenty blackbirds baked in a pie."

Four-and-Twenty Blackbird Pins

Here is what you need:

hole punch

paper fastener

scissors

two 6-inch (15-cm) paper bowls

black marker

seed beads

newspaper to work on

24 bird-shaped jigsaw puzzle pieces

white glue

yellow and black poster paint and a paintbrush

24 pin backs

aluminum foil

orange construction paper

modeling clay

Here is what you do:

1 Paint both sides of one bowl yellow for the top of the pie.

2 Cover the bottom of the second bowl with aluminum foil for the bottom of the pie.

3 Punch a hole in the edge of both bowls. Use the paper fastener to attach the top of the pie to the bottom.

HOLES

4 Use the marker to draw slits in the top of the pie.

PIE TOP

CUT LINES

BEADS FOR EYES

5 To make each blackbird, paint the plain side of each puzzle piece black.

Black

6 Give the round head of each bird a tiny triangle beak cut from the orange paper and two seed bead eyes, attaching them with glue.

7 Glue a pin back to the back of each bird.

8 Press clay over the bottom of the inside of the pie. Stand the 24 blackbirds in the clay and close the pie.

This project is perfect for a class or large group to make. Each person can make a blackbird to display in the pie and later take home to wear.

"Little Boy Blue come blow your horn."

Horn-Blowing Boy Blue

Here is what you need:

newspaper

9-inch (23-cm) uncoated paper plate

poster paint and a paintbrush in the skin tone of your choice

blue and red large office sticker dots

yarn for hair

white glue

party horn

aluminum foil

pencil

construction paper in blue and in skin tone for face

scissors

Here is what you do:

1 Paint the back of the plate for the head of Little Boy Blue.

2 Stick on two blue dots for eyes and a red dot for the nose. Glue yarn at the top for hair. Poke a small hole in the plate where the mouth should be to insert the blower end of the party horn.

PUNCH HOLE WITH PENCIL

WRAP

SIDE VIEW

3 Cover the cardboard part of the horn with aluminum foil. Put the blower end of the horn through the hole in the plate so that it looks like the horn is in front of the mouth.

FOLD IN HALF TO GET 2 HANDS. THEN TURN 1 HAND FACE DOWN

FOLD IN HALF TO GET 2 CUFFS

4 Trace your hands on the skin-tone paper. Cut the hand shapes out.

5 Cut a cuff for each hand from the blue paper. Glue a cuff to the wrist of each hand.

GLUE

6 Glue the cuffs on each side of the mouth with the hands folded up on the horn to look like they are holding it.

GLUE HERE

To make Little Boy Blue sound his horn just blow on the horn from behind the face.

"Humpty Dumpty had a great fall."

Roly-Poly Humpty Dumpty

Here is what you need:

clear plastic wrap

yellow clay or modeling compound

yarn

colored hole reinforcements

plastic egg that opens

scissors

large-size office sticker dots

GLUE white glue

thin ribbon

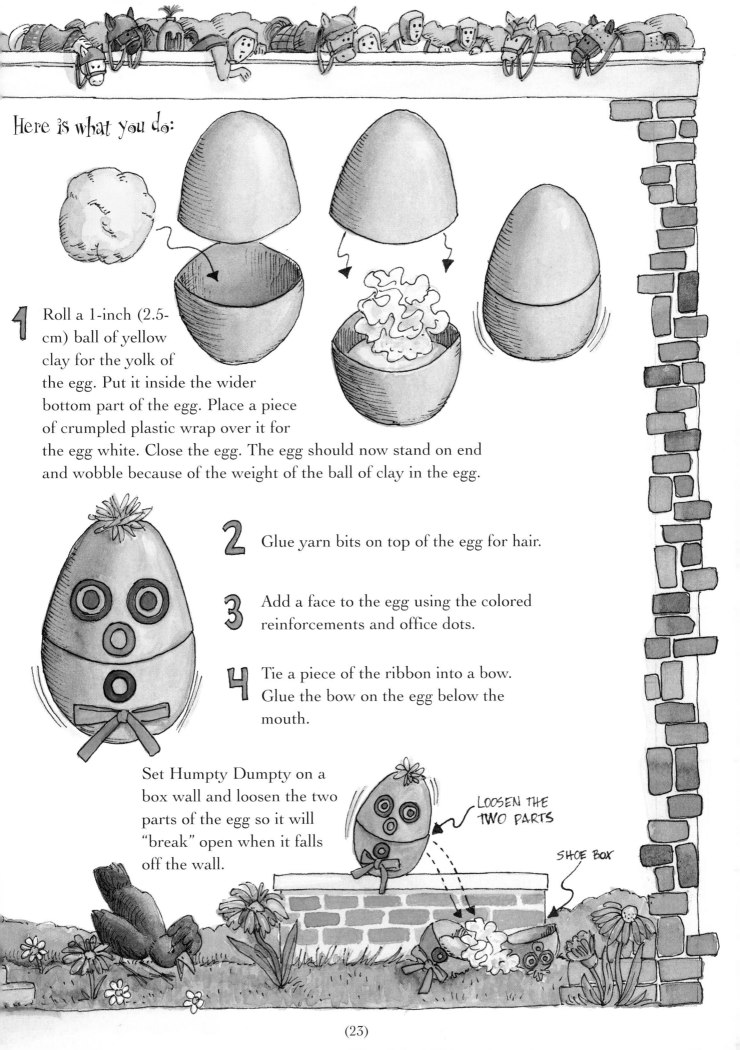

Here is what you do:

1 Roll a 1-inch (2.5-cm) ball of yellow clay for the yolk of the egg. Put it inside the wider bottom part of the egg. Place a piece of crumpled plastic wrap over it for the egg white. Close the egg. The egg should now stand on end and wobble because of the weight of the ball of clay in the egg.

2 Glue yarn bits on top of the egg for hair.

3 Add a face to the egg using the colored reinforcements and office dots.

4 Tie a piece of the ribbon into a bow. Glue the bow on the egg below the mouth.

Set Humpty Dumpty on a box wall and loosen the two parts of the egg so it will "break" open when it falls off the wall.

LOOSEN THE TWO PARTS

SHOE BOX

"Old Mother Hubbard went to
the cupboard to get her poor dog a bone."

Old Mother Hubbard's Dog

Here is what you need:

white glue

black film canister

two wiggle eyes

old stretchy glove

brown construction paper scrap

small brown pom-pom

brown and red pipe cleaners

scissors

fiberfill

Here is what you do:

1 The film canister will become the head for the dog, with the bottom of the canister his snout. Cut two ears from the brown paper. Glue an ear on each side of the canister.

CANISTER BOTTOM

FIDO

(24)

2 Glue the two wiggle eyes on the canister in front of the ears. Glue the pom-pom on the bottom of the canister for the nose.

FIBER FILL

3 Push enough fiberfill into the canister to make it fit snuggly on your finger.

4 Put the glove on your hand for the body of the dog. Cover the middle finger of the glove with glue, then position the canister with the eyes up and slide it onto your finger.

TAIL

POKE THROUGH GLOVE NEAR WRISTBAND. THEN TWIST OVER TO SECURE

5 Stick a piece of brown pipe cleaner through the glove at the opposite end from the head. Twist the end of the pipe cleaner around itself to secure it to the glove for a tail.

6 Wrap a piece of red pipe cleaner loosely around the neck of the dog and wrap the two ends together to make a collar.

ADD COLLAR

This dog puppet is so cute that if you make him sit up and beg, someone is sure to give him a bone.

"Hickity, Pickity, my black hen, she lays eggs for gentlemen."

Egg-Laying Black Hen

Here is what you need:

white glue

black craft feathers

old black stretchy glove

yellow and red rickrack trim

small plastic egg

two wiggle eyes

scissors

Here is what you do:

1 The thumb of the glove will be the head of the hen. Glue a wiggle eye on each side of the thumb.

2 Cut a point of yellow rickrack and glue it on the side of the thumb for the beak.

ATTACH ON THUMB TOP

ATTACH ON THUMB EDGE

SIDE #1   SIDE #2

3 Cut a strip of red rickrack to glue across the top of the thumb for the comb.

4 Glue the black craft feathers on both sides of the fingers.

5 Slip the plastic egg up inside the glove.

When you want the black hen to lay an egg, make lots of cackling sounds and gently squeeze the hen to work the egg out of the glove.

"And the dish ran away with the spoon."

Runaway Dish and Spoon Puppet

Here is what you need:

three 9-inch (23-cm) uncoated paper plates

newspaper to work on

poster paint and a paintbrush

two large and two small wiggle eyes

one large and one small pom-pom

pipe cleaners

yarn

ruler

scissors

white glue

plastic spoon

aluminum foil

cardboard paper towel tube

hole punch

Here is what you do:

1 Paint the eating side of one paper plate to look like a dinner plate.

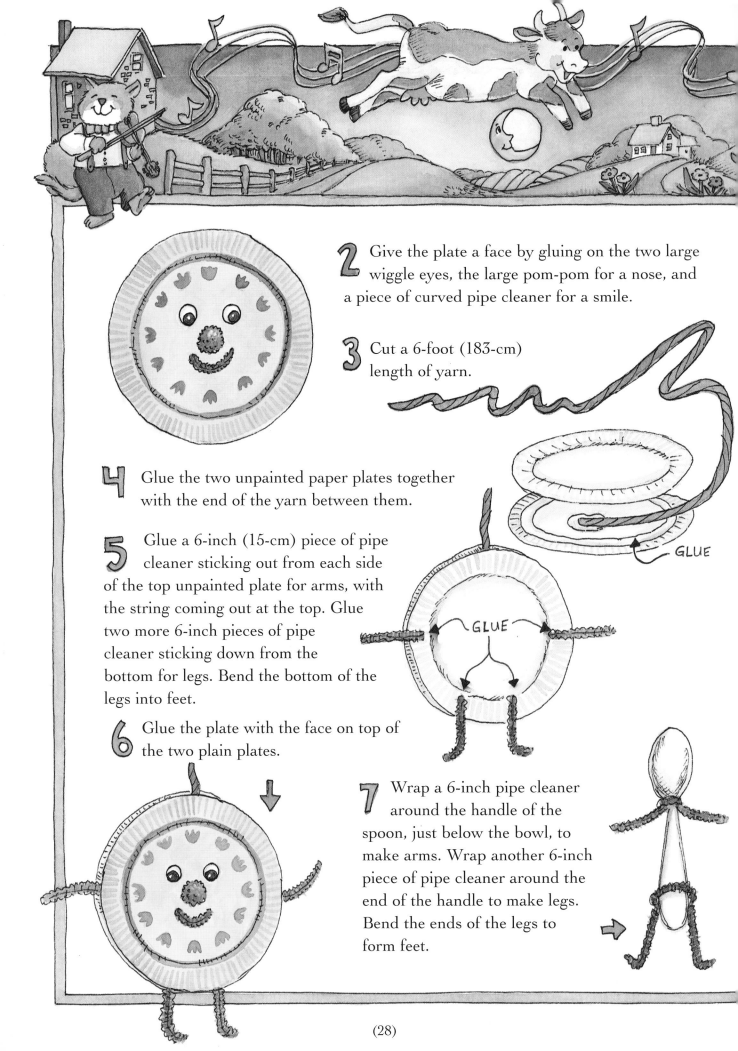

2 Give the plate a face by gluing on the two large wiggle eyes, the large pom-pom for a nose, and a piece of curved pipe cleaner for a smile.

3 Cut a 6-foot (183-cm) length of yarn.

4 Glue the two unpainted paper plates together with the end of the yarn between them.

5 Glue a 6-inch (15-cm) piece of pipe cleaner sticking out from each side of the top unpainted plate for arms, with the string coming out at the top. Glue two more 6-inch pieces of pipe cleaner sticking down from the bottom for legs. Bend the bottom of the legs into feet.

6 Glue the plate with the face on top of the two plain plates.

7 Wrap a 6-inch pipe cleaner around the handle of the spoon, just below the bowl, to make arms. Wrap another 6-inch piece of pipe cleaner around the end of the handle to make legs. Bend the ends of the legs to form feet.

GLUE

GLUE

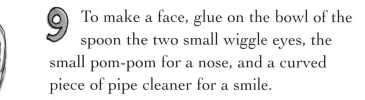

8 Cover the plastic spoon with aluminum foil, working around the arms and legs.

9 To make a face, glue on the bowl of the spoon the two small wiggle eyes, the small pom-pom for a nose, and a curved piece of pipe cleaner for a smile.

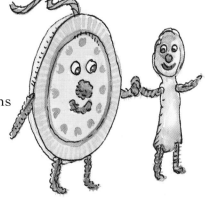

10 Join the dish and the spoon by wrapping their two pipe cleaner arms together at the ends to look like they are holding hands.

11 Punch a hole in the top and bottom edge of each side of the cardboard tube.

12 Thread the yarn up through both holes on one side of the tube and down through the other two holes on the opposite side. Tie the end of the yarn around the waist of the spoon, with the puppets at a height that is easy for you to work.

HOLES

THREAD YARN UP

13 Work the puppets by pulling on the yarn across the top of the tube.

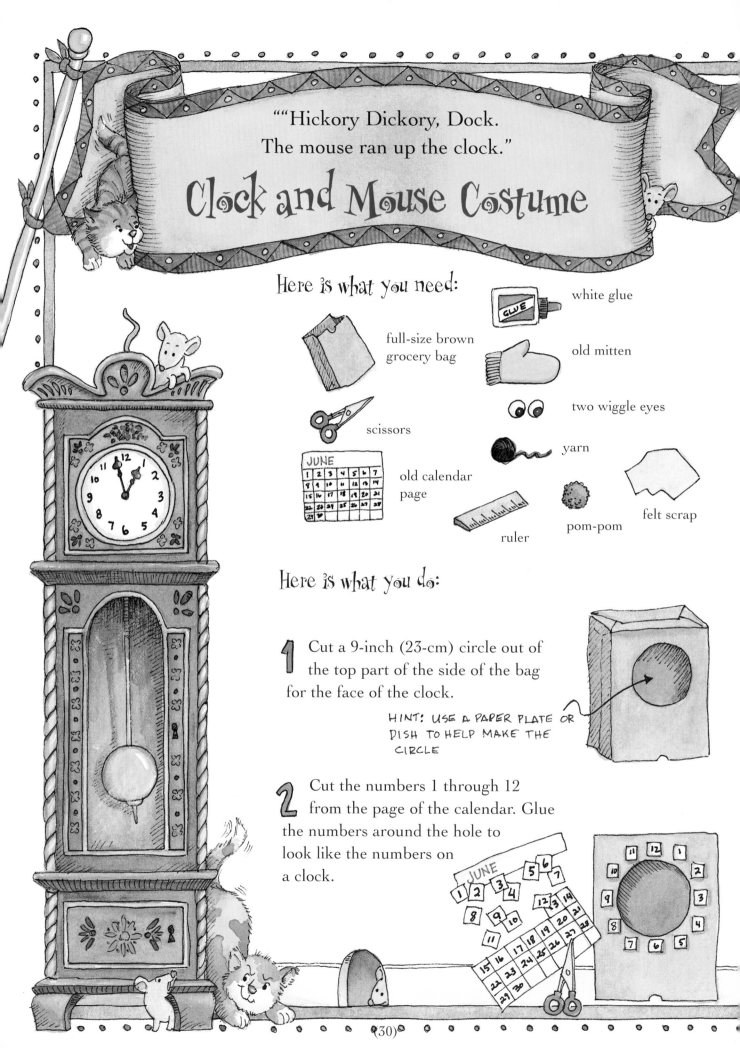

""Hickory Dickory, Dock.
The mouse ran up the clock."

Clock and Mouse Costume

Here is what you need:

full-size brown grocery bag

white glue

old mitten

scissors

two wiggle eyes

old calendar page

yarn

ruler

pom-pom

felt scrap

Here is what you do:

1. Cut a 9-inch (23-cm) circle out of the top part of the side of the bag for the face of the clock.

   HINT: USE A PAPER PLATE OR DISH TO HELP MAKE THE CIRCLE

2. Cut the numbers 1 through 12 from the page of the calendar. Glue the numbers around the hole to look like the numbers on a clock.

3 The mitten will become the mouse with the thumb forming the tail. Glue the two wiggle eyes on the end of the mitten on the thumb side.

4 Cut two 3-inch (8-cm) pieces of yarn. Glue the yarn to the top of the mitten, below the eyes, for the whiskers. Glue the pom-pom over the center of the whiskers for a nose.

5 Cut two 2-inch (5-cm) circles from the felt for the ears. Glue an ear on each side of the mitten.

YARN

TIC TOC TIC TOC

11 12 1
10 2
9 3
8 4
7 6 5

Put the bag clock on over your head so that your face becomes the face of the clock. Put the mitten mouse on your hand and run him up the clock and down again.

"Along came a spider and sat down beside her, and frightened Miss Muffet away."

Spider Car Antenna Friend

Here is what you need:

2-inch (5-cm) Styrofoam ball

discarded black panty hose

two thumbtacks

white glue

scissors

ballpoint pen

8 hairpins

Here is what you do:

1 Cut a leg off the panty hose.

CUT

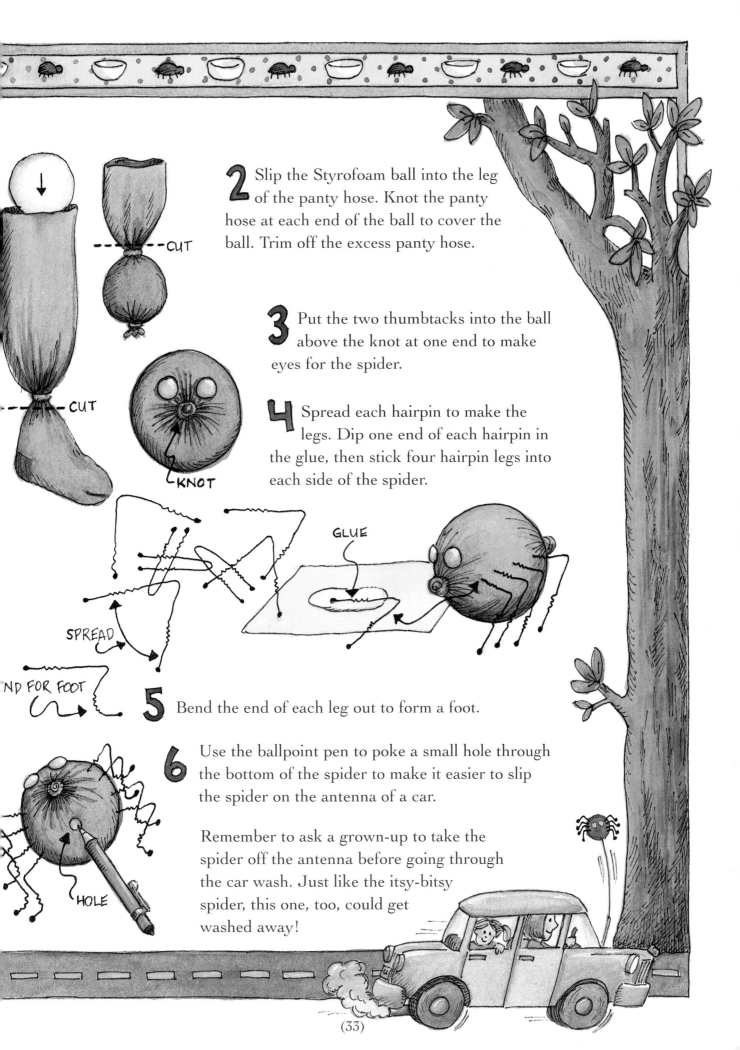

2 Slip the Styrofoam ball into the leg of the panty hose. Knot the panty hose at each end of the ball to cover the ball. Trim off the excess panty hose.

CUT

CUT

KNOT

3 Put the two thumbtacks into the ball above the knot at one end to make eyes for the spider.

4 Spread each hairpin to make the legs. Dip one end of each hairpin in the glue, then stick four hairpin legs into each side of the spider.

GLUE

SPREAD

ND FOR FOOT

5 Bend the end of each leg out to form a foot.

6 Use the ballpoint pen to poke a small hole through the bottom of the spider to make it easier to slip the spider on the antenna of a car.

Remember to ask a grown-up to take the spider off the antenna before going through the car wash. Just like the itsy-bitsy spider, this one, too, could get washed away!

HOLE

"The Knave of Hearts, he stole those tarts, and took them clean away."

Tart-Stealing Knave

Here is what you need:

white glue

paper clip

four red craft beads

masking tape

aluminum foil

old deck of cards

two craft sticks

sticky-back magnet

Here is what you do:

1 Wrap the bottom and sides of each of the red beads in a tiny piece of aluminum foil so that they look like berry tarts in tiny tins.

2 Shape a folded piece of foil into a tray to hold the tarts. Glue the tarts on the tray.

GLUE

3 Glue one end of the paper clip to the bottom of the tray so that it sticks out on one side. Secure the glued paper clip with a piece of masking tape.

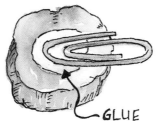

GLUE

GLUE TOGETHER

4 To make the queen puppet, glue a queen of hearts card to a second card with the end of a craft stick between them so that it sticks out from the bottom of the card for a holder.

5 Make the knave puppet in the same way using the knave of hearts card.

6 Set the queen and knave puppets down next to each other. Put a square of sticky-back magnet on the center of the inside edge of the card. Put a 2-inch (5-cm) strip of sticky-back magnet sticking out like an arm from the inside edge of the knave.

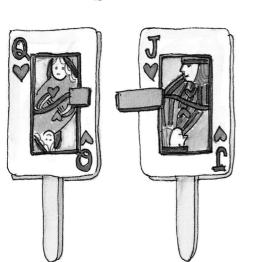

To use the puppets, stick the tarts on the magnet on the queen with the paper clip sticking out the side. Have the knave of hearts puppet sneak up and grab the tarts by the paper clip with the magnetic arm, so that the tarts stick to the arm. Then he should run away!

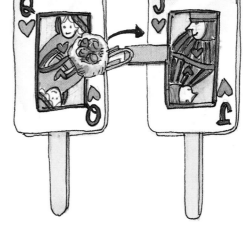

"Old King Cole was a merry old soul."

Old King Cole's Crown

Here is what you need:

colored plastic tape

scissors

white glue

pony craft beads

8-inch (20-cm) aluminum pie tin

Here is what you do:

1 Cut across the center of the pie tin without cutting the edges. Cut across the tin again to make four equal sections. Cut each section in half, but do not cut through the rim of the tin.

CENTER CUT

CUT 4 PARTS

| 1 | 2 |
| 3 | 4 |

CUT 8 PARTS

LIFT UP

2 Turn the tin upside down. Fold up all the sections of the cut tin to form to points of the crown.

FOLD TAPE OVER EDGE

3 Most pie tins are quite flimsy now, but if you have a sturdy pie tin that seems to have sharp edges, cover the cut edges with colored plastic tape.

4 Glue a pony bead on each point.

Put on the crown and call for your pipe, your bowl, and your fiddlers three.

"With silver bells and cockleshells
and pretty maids all in a row."

Mistress Mary's Bouquet

Here is what you need:

green pipe cleaners

ribbon

construction paper scraps

photographs or greeting cards with girls' faces

large plastic cap from laundry bottle

scissors

jingle bells

artificial flowers

white glue

shells

Here is what you do:

1 To make each "pretty maid" flower cut two 3-inch (8-cm) circles from construction paper. Cut 1-inch (2.5-cm) slits around the outside of the circles. Fold the cut sections of the two circles forward to look like the petals of a flower.

FOLD PETALS FORWARD

CUT LINES

SIDE VIEW

Cockle Shells

Silver Bells

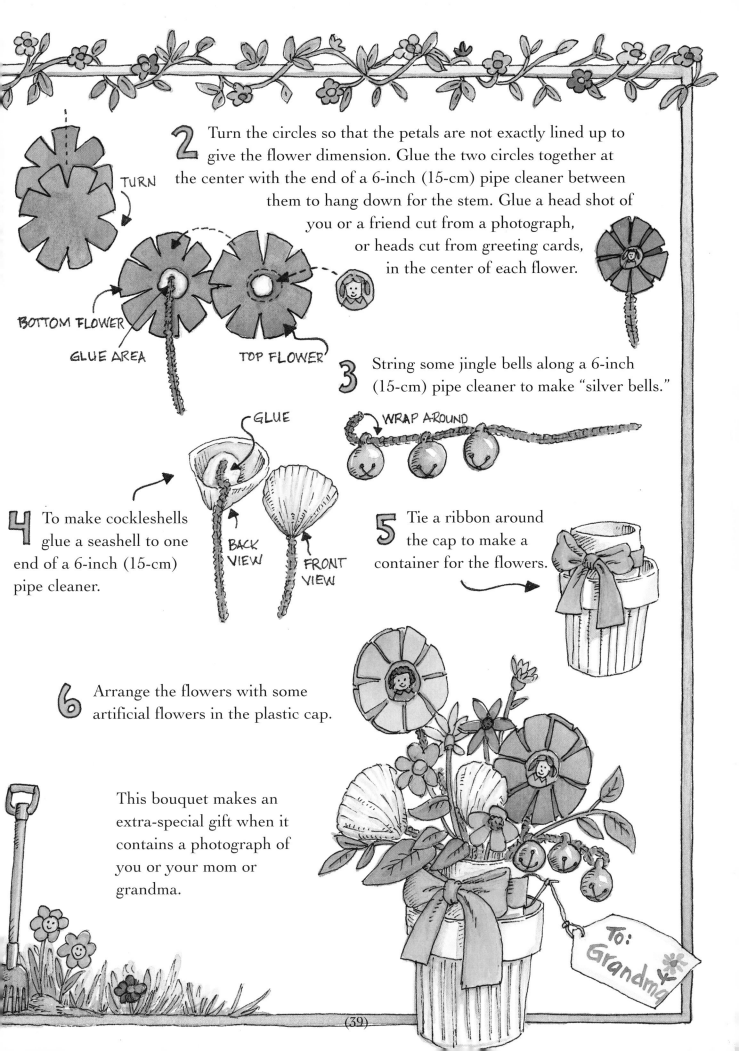

2 Turn the circles so that the petals are not exactly lined up to give the flower dimension. Glue the two circles together at the center with the end of a 6-inch (15-cm) pipe cleaner between them to hang down for the stem. Glue a head shot of you or a friend cut from a photograph, or heads cut from greeting cards, in the center of each flower.

TURN

BOTTOM FLOWER

GLUE AREA

TOP FLOWER

3 String some jingle bells along a 6-inch (15-cm) pipe cleaner to make "silver bells."

WRAP AROUND

GLUE

BACK VIEW

FRONT VIEW

4 To make cockleshells glue a seashell to one end of a 6-inch (15-cm) pipe cleaner.

5 Tie a ribbon around the cap to make a container for the flowers.

6 Arrange the flowers with some artificial flowers in the plastic cap.

This bouquet makes an extra-special gift when it contains a photograph of you or your mom or grandma.

To: Grandma

"Three little kittens lost
their mittens and they began to cry."

Crying Kitten Soap Dispenser

Here is what you need:

Styrofoam meat tray

two pump bottles of clear soap

ruler

jingle bell

scissors

pipe cleaner

two rubber bands

black permanent marker

flexi-straw

black trash bag

Here is what you do:

1 Hold the two soap pumps together with a rubber band with the spouts pointing sideways.

2 Wrap both bottles in a large piece of trash bag, with the spouts poked through, and held in place under the spouts with a rubber band.

TUCK UNDER

POKE SPOUTS THROUGH PLASTIC & WRAP OVER TO BACK. TUCK INTO RUBBER BAND

3 Cut a 4-inch (10-cm) circle from the Styrofoam tray for the head of the kitten. Cut two triangle ears from the top of the head.

CUT FOR EARS

4 Press the two spouts through the back of the head at about where the bottom of eyes will be on the face. Take the head off again.

SPOUTS

5 Use the marker to give the kitten a face.

HOLES

6 Thread the jingle bell on a 6-inch (15-cm) pipe cleaner and wrap the two ends together to make a collar for the kitten. Hang the collar over the two spouts so that the jingle bell hangs down in front of the spouts.

WRAP ENDS

7 Put the head back on by poking the two spouts through the two holes in the face.

8 Poke the bottom end of the flexi-straw through the back of the trash-bag covering, between the two bottles of soap, so that the bent end of the straw sticks up to form a tail.

Every time you wash your hands the kitten will "cry." Meeeeow, meeeeow!

"He stuck in his thumb and pulled out a plum."

Pull Out a Plum From the Pie

PLUM

Here is what you need:

- newspaper
- two 9-inch (23-cm) uncoated paper plates
- yellow poster paint and a paintbrush
- ruler
- scissors
- pencil
- construction paper in purple, red, green, and the skin tone of your choice
- white glue
- paper fastener
- trim

Here is what you do:

1 Paint the bottom (not the eating side) of one paper plate yellow for the top piecrust.

YELLOW

PLATE BOTTOM

PING PONG

2 Cut a 6-inch (15-cm) slit across the center of the piecrust.

CUT

3 Trace your hand on the skin-tone paper. Cut the hand out.

4 Cut an oval plum from the purple paper. Glue the plum to the thumb of the paper hand.

CUT

5 Attach the hand to the plate with the paper fastener so that the hand will swing up and down to slip the plum in and out of the slit cut in the pie.

SLIT

SWING

UNDER SLIT

6 Cut a 4-inch (10-cm) square of paper for a shirt cuff. Glue the edge of the cuff to the hand without gluing the paper fastener.

CUT CUFF

GLUE SPACE UNDER CUFF

7 Decorate the cuff by gluing trim at the wrist.

8 Cut two holly leaves from the green paper and some berries from the red paper. Glue the holly leaves together below the cut in the pie. Glue on the berries where the leaves meet.

Pull a plum out of the Christmas pie. Yum-yum!

GLUE LEAVES & BERRIES

GLUE

GLUE 2ND PLATE ALONG EDGE TO FORM PIE PAN

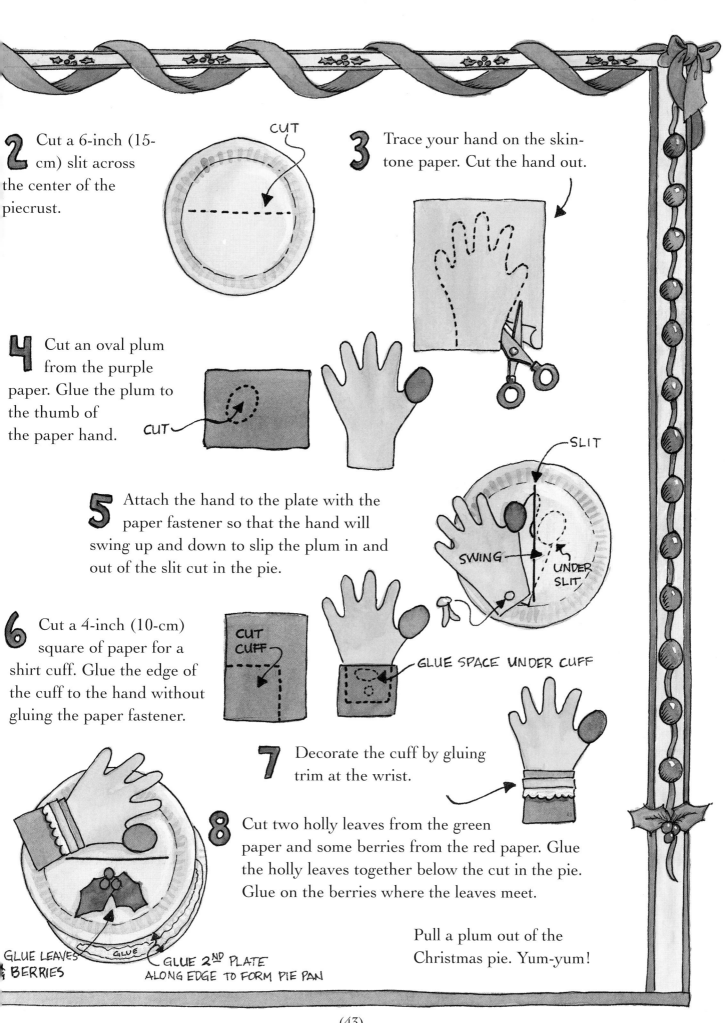

"Wee Willie Winkie runs through the town . . ."

Wee Willie Winkie Nightcap

Here is what you need:

discarded adult-size tights or leggings

scissors

pipe cleaner

jingle bell

white glue

Here is what you do:

1 Cut one leg off the leggings or tights. If you are using tights, cut the foot off the other end. Trim the leg to the length you want the nightcap to be.

CUT HERE

STRING BELL

ANKLE END

WRAP PIPE CLEANER HERE

2 Close the leg at the ankle, using a piece of pipe cleaner with a jingle bell strung on it.

3 Fold up the other end of the leg twice. Secure the fold with small dots of glue in four places around the folded rim. Do not use too much glue or the cap will not stretch to fit over your head.

FOLD TWICE

GLUE SPOTS UNDER FOLD

Do you know why people wore nightcaps a long time ago?

"1, 2, 3, 4, 5. I caught a fish alive!
6, 7, 8, 9, 10. Then I let him go again!"

Key Fish Magnet

Here is what you need:

old keys

craft paint

paintbrush

white glue

GLUE

small wiggle eyes

sequins

sticky-back magnet

Styrofoam tray to work on

Here is what you do:

1 Turn the key sideways so that the handle becomes the head of the fish and the notched end the tail. Paint one side of the key and let it dry on the Styrofoam tray.

2 Glue the wiggle eye to the head of the fish, covering the hole in the key if it has one.

GLUE ON THE UNDER SIDE

3 Glue the sequin to the back of the top of the key so that it sticks out to look like a mouth.

4 Put a piece of sticky-back magnet on the back of the fish.

Make several key fish to swim on your refrigerator. Bubble, bubble!

Pick up Pizza

Teacher Meeting!

Call Mom!

About the Author and Artist

Twenty-five years as a teacher and director of nursery-school programs have given Kathy Ross extensive experience in guiding young children through craft projects. Among the more than thirty-five craft books she has written are CRAFTS FOR ALL SEASONS, MAKE YOURSELF A MONSTER, THE BEST BIRTHDAY PARTIES EVER, CRAFTS FROM YOUR FAVORITE FAIRY TALES, CRAFTS FROM YOUR FAVORITE CHILDREN'S SONGS, and CRAFTS FROM YOUR FAVORITE CHILDREN'S STORIES.

Elaine Garvin designs and illustrates greeting cards and she has illustrated more than twenty children's books over the past ten years. A member of the Society of Children's Book Writers and Illustrators and the Graphic Artists Guild, she lives and works in Taunton, Massachusetts.

If you would like to know more about the author or the artist of this book, visit the Internet.

www.kathyross.com
www.elainegarvin.com